T0197398

The Gift
of
Amazing Grace

—— *Living Prayer Series*: Book 2 ——

Your prayer is my prayer too.
Karen Drucker

Christine Black Cummings
Illustrated by Lissa Evans

Balboa Press books may be ordered through booksellers or by contacting:

Balboa Press
A Division of Hay House
1663 Liberty Drive
Bloomington, IN 47403
www.balboapress.com
844-682-1282

Because of the dynamic nature of the Internet, any web addresses or links contained in this book may have changed since publication and may no longer be valid. The views expressed in this work are solely those of the author and do not necessarily reflect the views of the publisher, and the publisher hereby disclaims any responsibility for them.

Scripture quotations marked NLV are taken from the New Life Version, copyright © 1969 and 2003. Used by permission of Barbour Publishing, Inc., Uhrichsville, Ohio 44683. All rights reserved.

Photographs by Lissa Evans

ISBN: 978-1-9822-7800-7 (sc)
ISBN: 978-1-9822-7801-4 (e)

Print information available on the last page.

Balboa Press rev. date: 08/18/2022

Gratefully Dedicated to Rev. Marian Whiteman and Dr. Joe Hooper

Amazing Grace—via my Sedona friend Meredith Shay—introduced me to what is now *The Spiritual Center of the Desert*, Palm Desert, CA and its life-changing Philosophy of Life. There, I was **Graced** to CONNECT with the remarkable **Rev. Marian Whiteman** who became a minister at 80 and whose Wisdom, Light, Love and Laugher **Graced** me in ways that continue to uplift and encourage me. She saw Light in me that I didn't see, prayed and inspired me to complete and publish the account of my journey to wholeness: *Black-Eyed Susan, A Love-Child Finds Her Father and Her Self,* Balboa Press, 2013. I am forever grateful that The Master Weaver wove Rev. Marian's Golden Thread into the tapestry of my life.

As her **Amazing**, artistic, illustrator daughter Lissa Evans notes:

"When Reverend (Grammy) Marian Whiteman died in November 2019, she was remembered for her excellence in spiritual and grief counseling. Those in her inner circle knew her *Amazing Grace* to be her ability to honor the divine in others and bring out their true creative beauty. **A comment was made, "Grammy, how is it that when I walk in the room, you are always smiling and spreading joy?" Her response was, "I am just a reflection of you."**

———

This book is dedicated to Marian—**a celebration of her life of love**—as a teacher, poet, chaplain, minister, mother, author, healer, and kindred soul.

———

Dr. Joe Hooper, retired Spiritual Director of *The Center for Spiritual Living*, Palm Desert, shared a rock-solid bond with Rev. Marian for over 20 years.Their dynamic energy would light up our spiritual home as they CONNECTed and shared their **Amazing** gifts.

Dr. Joe's *Rainbow of God Attributes Meditation* was my original inspiration for what became ***The Gift of Amazing Grace.*** The words of this ***Living Prayer*** follow the steps of Affirmative Prayer that were part of my study to become a Prayer Practitioner and that remain part of my daily spiritual practice.

———

This book is dedicated to Dr. Joe, for his bountiful legacy that continues to bless and prosper me and the many others whose lives are forever reframed and changed in **Amazing** ways thanks to his leadership of love and service. Blessings on your well-deserved retirement and new adventures.

Gratitudes

To all who have inspired me, and to you and others
who have accompanied me on my spiritual journey, thank you.
To others who love and support me in so many other ways
—especially you, my beloved Dave—
I gratefully appreciate each of you.
To all my believers and encouragers,
my grateful heart overflows to each of you.
To the Spiritual Center of the Desert, Palm Desert, CA
—especially Rev. Dale Olansky and Dr. Laura Shackelford—
I appreciate the Light you shine and for being my spiritual home.
Thank you, Dr. James Mellon, our Spiritual Leader, for uplifting me and others to
"Love Only - Forgive Everything - Remember Who You Are" and **"Do It Now!"**
And to know: **"Wherever I Am, God Is."**
For daily email inspiration from Dr. Maxine Kaye, Alan Cohen, Neale Donald Walsch,
Rev. Christian Sorensen, Unity's *Daily* Word and also Sarah Young's *Jesus Calling*,
plus Karen Drucker, Daniel Nahmod, Karl Anthony and other spiritual singers
and empowering retreat/workshop/"play shop" leaders:
in Karen's words: *I am so grateful, I am so blessed.*
I appreciate all in Unity's *Daily Word* 7 AM Meditation Circle I lead at Chaparral Country
Club for their sharing, caring, prayers, love and laughter.
Thank you, Mary Ellen Peterson, for gracing me with the colorful prayer shawl that
now graces the Pocket Prayer at the end of this book.
And for my amazing 8 AM Prayer Partner Suzanne Stradley, gratitude abounds.
Thank you Mom (*Mor-Mor* to many) for teaching me that getting up early is a gift.
You are a gift whose life and legacy continue to inspire.

And to YOU who are reading this, I am grateful for you.

Lissa Evans is best known for her "Intimate Landscapes" which capture simple and effortless beauty. Her goal is to change the way people look at the planet, to see without assumptions.

With her workshops and powerful video, "The Salton Sea: A Sea Out of Focus", she advocates for California's rapidly changing Salton Sea. Lissa's photography has been featured in art publications, a film, book covers and commercial websites.

Lissa has garnered numerous awards including Best of Show and People's Choice. Lissa lives with her husband at Two Mountain Studios near Palm Springs, CA.

———

Amazing, gifted and giving Lissa entered my life via her mother, Rev. Marian Whiteman, joining my circle of beloved friends after she and husband Kirk moved to the Coachella Valley to be closer to her then aging mother. Several years later, **Amazing Grace** found the perfect home in my Chaparral County Club neighborhood for Grammy and her then caregiver niece, another beloved friend, Missy Jones.

As we've collaborated on this book, Lissa's artwork and her ideas that bubble up keep bringing me pure JOY. I once wrote to her mother: "Spending time with you always feels like I've gotten to the POT of GOLD at the end of the rainbow." Lissa, my friend, the POT of GOLD is YOU!!! Gratitude and love abound.

Table of Contents

In my awakening, I find God, I find myself.
Karl Anthony

God Is…I Am…We are One

There is a presence, power, and creative energy that is all and only good.
It is infinite intelligence, limitless abundance,
health, wholeness, peace and unconditional love.
Everywhere present and available at all times, It is equally accessible to all.
I call that power God.

God is my source, I am God's expression; we are inseparably one.

God provides everything I require to live a life that is
prosperous, joyful, healthy, peaceful and purposeful.

It is a life of love and service. That life is my life now.

I Am Ready

I release anything that restricts me from receiving God's gifts
and using them to live that life and to share my blessings with the world.

I am ready to receive, share and soar.

Abundance

I receive and share with gratitude the
Abundance that is God and I prosper.
I receive gratefully, use consciously and joyfully, share generously.
Abundantly blessed, we bless and prosper
ourselves, others and our world.
God's bounty, wisdom and inspiration flow to and through each of us
in a perfect circle of giving and receiving,
expanding to bless the world and returning in miraculous multiples.

In the flow of Amazing Grace, our cups overflow.

We are the heart, we are the hands, we are the voice of Spirit on earth.
And who we are and all we do is a blessing to the world.
Karen Drucker

Power

I gratefully receive and recirculate the **Power** that is God
and I am energized.
God's **Power** fuels our passion, ignites our creativity
and inspires us to take action.
Connected to our **Power** Source,
we create a circuitry to God-energy that weaves a worldwide web.

God-Powered, we soar.

*There's One Power, invisible, and you see it everywhere and every
day...whatever name you give it, it's all One Power, can't you see?
It's the power of the love in you and me.*
Daniel Nahmod

Life

I gratefully receive and share the **Life** that is God and all is well.
Our spirits, minds and bodies
—and all our cells, parts, organs and systems—
are in perfect health, balance and flow.
As we nurture our minds, bodies and spirits
with **Life**-giving thoughts, food, fluids, activity and rest,
our healthy lifestyles inspire others.

In divine well-being, we thrive.

I am healed whole and healthy.
I am well.
Karen Drucker

Light

I gratefully receive and share the **Light** that is God and I glow.
The **Light** that we shine **light**s our pathway and our world,
glorifying the **Light** of the world.
Like moths to a flame, our God-**Light**
attracts others who are ready to be more en**light**ened.
Bright as shining stars,
our God glow glimmers wherever we go.

In God's Holy Light, our world is aglow.

Let it shine, let it shine,
I let my big bright brilliant beam of radiant light shine.
Karen Drucker

Beauty

I gratefully receive and share the **Beauty** that is God and I bloom.

We are all God's beautiful creations,

sprouting, growing, blossoming

into ever more beautiful expressions

of who we are created to be.

Appreciating the **Beauty,** order, balance and diversity of Nature,

I am One with all God's beautiful creations.

Together, we plant the seeds and pull the weeds

that grow God's garden into **Beauty** that knows no bounds.

In the Beauty of diversity, Love blossoms.

How could anyone ever tell you,
you were anything less than beautiful?
Libby Roderick

Joy

I gratefully receive and share the **Joy** that is God and I am radiant.
As bliss bubbles up in us, we sing on key and dance to the beat
of this glorious gift that is our life.
We sizzle with zest and enthusiasm to be who we are created to be
and to live the lives we are designed to live.
Spreading **Joy**, we join others in chorus lines of songs and dances
that make the world a happier place.

Blissfully blessed, Joy fills our world.

Joy fills every cell of my body, every cell is alive with love.
Karen Drucker

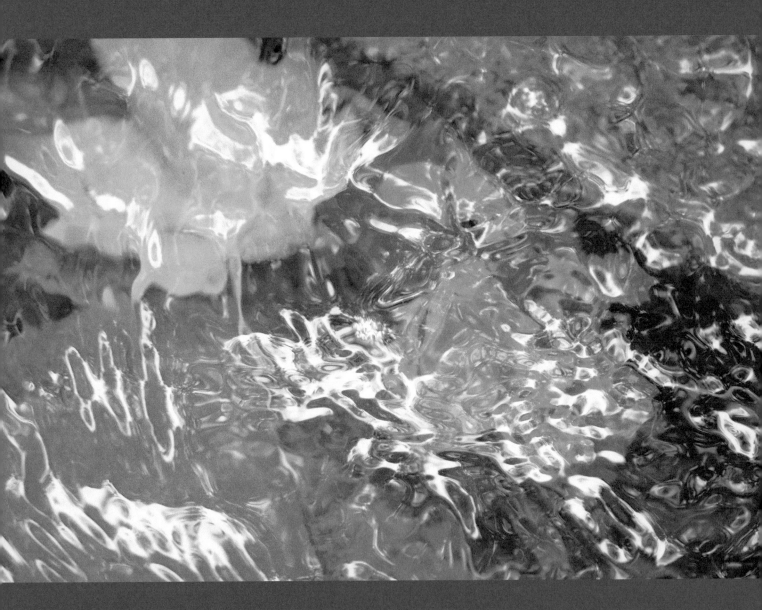

Peace

I gratefully receive and recirculate the **Peace** that is God and I am free.
Surrendered to divine wisdom and **Amazing Grace**,
we are harmonious within ourselves
and in our relationships and experiences.
Forgiving what was, accepting what is
and embracing what is next and beyond,
we connect in community
to weave a tapestry of **Peace** that blankets the world.

In Oneness, Peace prevails.

Let there be peace on earth, and let it begin with me.
Jan Jackson-Miller

Love

I gratefully receive and share the **Love** that is God
and I am loved, lovable and loving.
Each one of us is a child of God's **Love**,
conceived and created to express the **Love** that brought us into being
and evolving into a fuller expression of that **Love**.
Our loving hearts see and celebrate the face of God
in all children of God's **Love**. Brothers and sisters all,
we reach out, one to another, joining hands
in an endless and ever-expanding circle
of the **Love** of our Creator and that is our reason for being.

And the greatest of these is Love.
1 Corinthians 13:13

Love is my decision,
my decision right here and now.
Danial Nahmod

Gratitude

I breathe in Peace and am filled with **Gratitude** that I am so well supplied
and that further replenishment and refreshment are as near
as my next conscious breath, my next God-inspired thought.
Awake to my potential, alive with possibilities,
I celebrate, enjoy and share *The Gift of Who I Am*
and the glorious God-gifts that grace my life.

I am so grateful. I am so blessed.
Karen Drucker

Release

Grateful to be God's beautiful expression
beautifully expressing
and for the Power within that does the work,
I **release** this prayer with joyous expectancy
that **Amazing Grace** shows up all over the place
for all God's beloved creations, now and forevermore.
Letting go and letting God, I let it be.
And so it is.

Speaking words of wisdom, let it be, let it be.
Paul McCartney

My Personal Reflections

As you reflect on *The Gift of Amazing Grace,* ask yourself: When **something greater** speaks, am I listening?
As I listen, do I hear? As I hear, am I open to receive?
As I receive, do I use the gifts I receive in ways that benefit and prosper me and others too?

This page is for **your** Personal Reflections

_____

_____

_____

_____

_____

_____

_____

_____

_____

_____

_____

_____

_____

_____

_____

_____

My Living Prayers

My prayer is that this ***Living Prayer*** helps you find new ways
to live with ease and grace and to live and give more joyfully and generously.

This page is for **your** Living Prayers for yourself, others and our world.

_____

_____

_____

_____

_____

_____

_____

_____

_____

_____

_____

_____

_____

_____

_____

_____

_____

_____

_____

Amazing Grace Pocket Prayer

There is a Power for Good that I call God.
It lives in, as and through me. We are inseparably One.

God provides everything I require to thrive.
In faith and trust, I am ready to receive, share and soar.

As I gratefully receive and share the **Abundance** that is God,
Amazing Grace blesses and prospers all.

I gratefully receive and share the **Power** that is God.
God-**Power**ed, we soar.

I gratefully receive and share the **Life** that is God and all is well.
In divine well-being, we thrive.

I gratefully receive and share the **Light** that is God and we shine.
In God's holy **Light**, our world is aglow.

I gratefully receive and share the **Beauty** that is God and we bloom.
In the **Beauty** of diversity, **Love** blossoms.

As I gratefully receive and share the **Joy** that is God, we are radiant.
Blissfully blessed, **Joy** fills our world.

I gratefully receive, share and surrender to the **Peace** that is God,
affirming that we are Free to live in **Peace** and unity.
In the Oneness of community, **Peace** prevails.

I gratefully receive and share the **Love** that is God,
acknowledging we are all expressions of God's **Love**,
showing up in our own uniquely gifted ways.

I breathe gratitude that I am so well supplied.
May others receive and benefit from this prayer.

With joyous expectancy, I release this prayer.
As I let go, let God, I let it be. And so it is.

And the greatest of these is Love.
1 Corinthians 13:13

My gratitude abounds to these **amazing** musically gifted gifts to the world whose lyrics now **grace** this Living Prayer. It is my prayer that you explore more of their music and that it will inspire, uplight, accelerate your healing and **grace** your life in **amazing** ways.

Karen Drucker: www.karendrucker.com

Karen's message is all about healing and love – whether singing one of her positive message songs or sharing stories that are funny, inspiring, and heart opening. She is a keynote speaker at mind-body and health conferences, women's retreat facilitator, webinar leader and entertainer who has recorded 22 CDs of her inspirational music. Her chants and songs are used around the world, helping people deal with illness and loss or filling their need to feel more centered for the day.

Karen is also the author of the best selling book *Let Go of the Shore - Songs & Stories To Set The Spirit Free.*

Karen loves making music and her intention is to make a difference by using her music to open hearts and share a message of hope, acceptance, and love. Her music is used for people going through cancer treatments, by workshops leaders, authors and people who tell her that her music inspires and comforts them.

Karen with Diane Berk and me at *The Call of Something More* Retreat at Asilomar

Daniel Nahmod: www.danielnahmod.com

Singer/Songwriter, producer and humanitarian Daniel Nahmod (pronounced Nay-mod) has performed his profound, heart-opening original music for over one million people since beginning his music career in 1999. His songs are recorded and performed all over the world and Daniel has presented his spectacular music and message for nearly all of the world's major faiths. His poetic and evocative message of peace, love and compassion across all nations, cultures and faiths has found overwhelming acceptance. In addition to his performances, Daniel facilitates retreats and offers his uplifting, informative weekly *Musical Mondays* on Facebook Daniel Nahmod USA.

Daniel with Diane Berk and me at a *Water* Retreat in Scottsdale, AZ

Karl Anthony: www.karlanthony.com

Karl speaks, sings, writes, consults, produces and advocates for the arts in healthcare and facilitates international service tours around the world, now in places like Thailand. His biggest joy is collaborating with others who wish to make a difference in the world and an impact in our communities. In his words: "Let's create something **amazing** together."

Libby Roderick: www.libbyroderick.com

Printed in the United States
by Baker & Taylor Publisher Services